BUILDING YOUR FINANCIAL FUTURE FROM THE PRESENT

TABLE OF CONTENTS

PROLOGUE 4

BUILDING YOUR FINANCIAL FUTURE FROM THE PRESENT 5

CHAPTER 1 : BENEFITS OF HAVING A TAX-FREE STRATEGY FOR RETIREMENT: 7

CHAPTER 2 : INTRODUCTION 11

CHAPTER 3 : RETIREMENT SAVINGSRETIREMENT SAVINGS STRATEGIES 17

Chapter 4 : Balancing Present Lifestyle With The Future 32

Chapter 5 : Bucket list 36

Chapter 6 : What we've been taught, against what is true: 42

Chapter 7 : Mastery over your finance 44

PROLOGUE

It is not coincidence that you are reading this now. I truly believe that when people are doing well, it creates abundance for everyone. This might be difficult to believe, since traditionally, the world doesn't think that what one man can do, another can do also.

I would like to say thank you to my wonderful family, my sweet mother, and my two amazing daughters, Catherine and Stephanie. I would also like to say a big thank you to Cesar R Lopez, my loving husband, for introducing me into the industry and teaching me the importance and purpose of our career; the purpose of changing the world by helping and protecting so many families the way we do.

LifePro Solutions is focused on creating and providing great care for you and ensuring that you meet your goals in life. LifePro Solutions also protects your money and makes you wealthy. The quality of our services is exceptional.

BUILDING YOUR FINANCIAL FUTURE FROM THE PRESENT

Retirement is a term that has been in usage for a long time and all it means is that you are no longer producing income. Usually it was used to refer to a person more than 55 year of age, but times have changed, and we are now facing a new age where we can balance lifestyles, manage time to our favor, and be more efficient by investing on what is important – as I always say, keep the main thing (THE MAIN THING), connect more with your purpose in life, with what you want to experience and live.

For great experiences, and usually for a creative bucket list, it is important to have control of your finances, and create a plan for learning instruments already in existence, with which you can make the most of every dollar you earn. The intention of this book is to start with a guide to the different names that have been given to plans, to understand their differences, and guide you into making the best decisions.

Here we go.... Enjoy the ride....

CHAPTER 1

BENEFITS OF HAVING A TAX-FREE STRATEGY FOR RETIREMENT:

Retirement will creep up on everyone at some point in their lives, yet so many seem quite unprepared for this reality that must surely come.

There are some people who do not realize that upon retirement, their accounts will be subject to being taxed, and when they do not prepare for being taxed, and the percentages of tax deductions that would eventually come, their expectations usually are cut short because their finances usually get exhausted much earlier than they had anticipated.

Typical retirement accounts, which include the IRAs and pre-tax 401(k)s or just traditional retirement accounts generally undergo tax deductions which are similar to regular income in accordance with the year in which it is received.

Taking all these into consideration, it becomes obvious that the most pronounced means of losing money in retirement is through tax deductions on retirement plans. Unfortunately, this comes at a time when your only means of sponsoring your lifestyle is dependent upon retirement savings, and no longer on your paycheck, unless you have social security or well-structured benefit pension plans in place.

Therefore, it goes to say that having a smart retirement strategy is very important if an individual is ever going to have a satisfactory retirement experience.

But how well thought out is your retirement plan?

Taking an example of qualified retirement plans like the

401(k)s and IRAs, and the likes of them; *the* retirement plans would let you contribute your retirement funds on a 'to-be-taxed-later' basis known as pre-tax, meaning you don't pay taxes on them right now, but later.

And it sounds cool and right.

Because the taxes you pay now on your now reduced income, out of which your tax contributions have been deduced, appears lower and it feels good at the moment.

This is what I refer to as the 'I'll Pay It Later' mindset.

But there is a little catch in this setup. Did I say little? Here's how it happens, after retirement, you begin to take your money out, and that's the time you would start making all the tax payment you deferred, and had not paid at the time of your contribution deductions, and you'll pay these taxes for as long as you take money, which could very likely mean for the rest of your life.

So basically, your retirement plan is either 'pre-tax' or 'after-tax'.

You may ask how much of a difference that would make?

Consider for example that you plan to invest a hundred thousand dollars into your chosen retirement plan, and you choose to go pre-tax, this means you're investing the whole of the hundred thousand dollars to be taxed later.

Should you opt for the after tax and place current tax rate

at 40%, you will have to withdraw $166,666 to pay taxes and keep $100,000 expendable for you.

So that, when you retire on the after-tax plan, your $100,000.00 is yours to withdraw WITHOUT ANY FURTHER PAYMENTS OF TAX OR CHARGES, quite unlike the former situation where you'll have to pay the influencing tax rate as long as your retirement lasts.

Another benefit of having an after-tax plan is the uncertainty of tax rate fluctuations.

What happens to your money if the prevailing tax rate during your retirement tips towards an increased taxation rate?

Obviously, that would mean much less money for you to withdraw, and could absolutely crush the retirement dreams of so many.

Do you think you can cope with that?

Sometimes it's not just about how much you're saving, but where and how you are making these retirement savings eventually make the difference.

CHAPTER 2

INTRODUCTION

RETIREMENT

Retirement means voluntary or forced withdrawal from active participation in a job or business.

Retirement is a time when a person no longer works, or the beginning of that period. In the United States, the standard age for retirement is 65, although sometimes people may decide to retire earlier or later due to personal or financial reasons, such as eligibility for private or public pension benefits. Also, some people semi-retire by reducing work hours.

WHAT IS FINANCIAL INDEPENDENCE

Financial independence means having enough personal wealth to live, without working actively for basic necessities.

Financial independence at retirement means having enough resources to live comfortably. Financial independence at retirement is unlikely when retirement planning is poorly done.

WHAT IS RETIREMENT PLANNING

Retirement planning like any other kind of planning means preparing every aspect of living for life at the end of paid work. Retirement planning involves deciding necessary income goals, actions, and decisions. It includes identifying sources of income, estimating expenses, lifestyle choices, savings, investment programs, managing assets, and estimating future cash flows. Retirement planning choices have been limited to choices that fall on either the safe part of the scale or the risky, but there are options with a big reward and less risk, which we would consider later. But for now, let's look into the types of retirement plans.

TYPES OF RETIREMENT PLANS

DEFINED BENEFIT PLAN

Defined benefit plan is based on future benefits that an employee receives which is affected by the individual's salary history and years of service. It is a specified monthly benefit promised at retirement which is paid from a trust fund dedicated to the plan.

DEFINED CONTRIBUTION PLAN

A defined contribution plan is an employer-sponsored plan in which benefits accrue only from contributions into the employee's individual account. These contributions are invested on the employee's behalf. The employee receives benefits based on investment gains subtracted from losses and expense charges. The employee's account is used to provide retirement benefits. The value of the account fluctuates due to changes in the value of the investments. Examples of defined contribution plans include employee stock ownership plans and profit-sharing plans.

SIMPLIFIED EMPLOYEES PENSIONS PLAN

Simplified Employee Pension Plan (SEP) allows tax-favored contributions to individual retirement accounts (IRAs) owned by the employees. SEPs are subject to minimal reporting and disclosure requirements. An employee is required to sets up an IRA into which payments are made by the employer. The contributions are made into the SEP, and it is not considered taxable income for employees, although employees will owe taxes when they make withdrawals from their accounts.

PROFIT SHARING PLAN OR STOCK BONUS PLAN

Profit Sharing Plan or Stock Bonus Plan is a contribution plan which provides or gives the employer the opportunity to choose annually how much will be contributed to the plan. The plan contains a formula for allocating to each participant, a portion of each annual contribution. A profit sharing plan or stock bonus plan includes the 401k plan

EMPLOYEE STOCK OWNERSHIP PLAN (ESOP)

Employee Stock Ownership Plan (ESOP) is a defined contribution plan in which the investments are primarily in employer stock.

MONEY PURCHASE PENSION PLAN

Money Purchase Pension Plan is a plan that requires fixed annual contributions from the employer to the employee's individual account. The plan is subject to certain funding rules and other rules.

CASH BALANCE PLAN

Cash Balance Plan delineates benefit similar to the Defined Contribution Plan. Cash balance plan defines promised benefit that comes in form of a stated account balance. The participant's account is credited each year with a pay credit and an interest credit. Increases and decreases in the value of the plan's investments do not directly affect the benefit amounts promised to participants. The investment risks and rewards on plan assets are solely borne by the employer. When a participant becomes entitled to receive benefits under a cash balance plan, the benefits received are defined in terms of an account balance. The benefits, usually in form of cash balance plans, and similar to most traditional defined benefit plans, are protected, within certain limitations, by federal insurance provided through the Pension Benefit Guaranty Corporation (PBGC).

NONQUALIFIED DEFERRED COMPENSATION

Employer agrees to pay select employees a defined amount of compensation at a future date.

WHAT IS AN IRA (INDIVIDUAL RETIREMENT ACCOUNT)?

The term IRA was repeated a number of times while discussing the types of retirement plans and it might have left you wondering what it means. IRA (Individual Retirement Account) is an account set up at a financial institution that allows an individual to save for retirement with tax-free growth or on a tax-deferred basis. IRA is an investment tool used by individuals to earn and set aside funds for retirement savings. There are several types of IRAs such as Traditional Individual Retirement Accounts, Nondeductible Traditional Individual Retirement Accounts, Roth Individual Retirement Accounts, Simple Individual

Retirement Accounts, and Simplified Employee Pension Individual Retirement Accounts.

HOW DOES AN IRA WORK?

To operate an IRA you need to open an account through an insurance company, employer, a bank, or a financial services firm. Then contributions can be made by depositing money from your savings periodically, through payroll deductions or by making a lump sum deposit. Most plans offer various funding options such as annuities, stocks, bonds and mutual funds. You become eligible to begin making withdrawals from the account when you are 59½ years old. Generally, there is a 10% penalty for withdrawing funds before you turn 59½.

CHAPTER 3

RETIREMENT SAVINGS STRATEGIES

TAX-DEFERRAL STRATEGY

A retirement plan in which a contributor does not pay taxes on contributions until after withdrawal at retirement. A portion of the pre-tax income is put into a retirement account for investment purposes. Taxation is deferred until withdrawal from the account following retirement. When retirement income is taken, taxes are due on the tax-deferred gain. The strategy entails deferring payment of income tax on money you save for retirement in a 401(k) and IRA.

TAX-FREE RETIREMENT INCOME

Tax-free Retirement Income entails setting aside a portion of tax income, so that earnings grow, tax-deferred. Income tax on money contributed to Roth IRA, permanent life insurance and Roth 401(k) will accrue without taxes while in the account. If withdrawals are made after age 59½ from an account that is at least 5 years old, tax will not be paid on the investment earnings. Retirement money is income tax-free.

AFTER TAX SAVING

Setting aside a portion of your taxable income into an account created for retirement. Taxes are paid annually on any earning.

PRE-TAX STRATEGY

Might include an employer-sponsored qualified plan, like a 401(k) and 403 (b) plan. You don't pay current tax on the contribution made to the plan, and earnings grow tax-deferred. Later when you take retirement income the benefits are income taxable.

THE MYRA.

A new type of Roth retirement account, the myRA, guarantees that savings will never decline in value. The only investment option is a Treasury savings bond that pays a variable interest rate. However, when investors accumulate $15,000 or the account turns 30 years old, savings will be transferred to a private sector.

ROTH IRA

TRUSTEE-TO-TRUSTEE TRANSFERS

A trustee-to-trustee transfer is when you transfer 401(k) to an IRA, or a new 401(k), or change jobs. You transfer your balance directly from one account to another via a trustee-to-trustee transfer. If a check is cut to you, 20 percent of your savings will be withheld for income tax. You are given 60 days to put the distribution, including the withheld 20 percent, in a new retirement account. If you don't meet the deadline you will owe income tax and potentially an early-withdrawal penalty on any amount that doesn't make it into another retirement account. A trustee-to-trustee transfer allows you to avoid the tax withholding and the potential to trigger taxes and fees.

TAX-FREE IRA CHARITABLE CONTRIBUTIONS

Withdrawals from traditional IRAs are required after age 70 1/2, and income tax is due on each distribution. Retirees who are 70 1/2 or older can avoid tax and fulfill their withdrawal requirement by directly transferring amounts of up to $100,000 from their IRA to a qualified charity, holding tax-preferred investments outside of retirement accounts.

Some types of investments receive preferential tax

treatment. Long-term capital gains are taxed at a lower rate than short-term gains and ordinary income. Investments that generate long-term capital gains in a traditional 401(k) or IRA, won't have to pay tax on it while it is in the account, but you will owe ordinary income tax on the investment gains when you withdraw from the account.

DIRECTLY DEPOSITING YOUR TAX REFUND TO AN IRA

Saving part of windfalls for retirement, including your tax refund, can help grow your retirement savings faster.

EMPLOYER CONTRIBUTION

Save to get any 401(k) by matching your employer offering. It is important to take a look at your company's vesting schedule to see if there are any job tenure requirements before you can take the 401(k) match when leaving your job.

MULTIPLE SAVINGS PLANS

The 2001 tax law repealed some of the rules that coordinated the various annual contribution limits for the different tax-deferred plans into one limit. What that means is that you may have the ability to save with more than one retirement plan at the same time. Contributions to different savings plans are no longer interdependent.

SMART TAX PLANNING

With the likely increase in tax rate, 410k and IRA are not the best places to save a large part of your retirement. You won't really know how much you are making because the Federal government gets to vote what percentage they get to keep. If you believe in the old laws that tax will be lower in retirement than working years, rethink it to reflect present happenings and stay on top of your game. Move payments from high taxable accounts to low taxable accounts, so that when taxes increase you can enjoy a reduction in retirement taxes. The good news however is that zero percent retirement tax planning is possible even as unrealistic as it seems.

HOW TO REALIZE ZERO PERCENT TAX ON RETIREMENT

ROTH IRA

Roth IRAis an account that allows Americans under 40 to contribute a maximum of $5,500 to a Roth IRA, or $6,500 if you are aged 50 or older by the end of the year, **and $11,000 for a couple**, or if you are single or the single head of a household and your Modified Adjusted Gross Income (**MAGI**) is less than $118,000. Roth IRAs are funded with after-tax dollars; the contributions are not **tax deductible**.

If you earn beyond the accepted limit you can still enjoy its benefits by converting from your IRA to Roth. A 28% tax will be charged for the shift which is 3% higher that IRA. The advantage here is that your money will be free from taxation. Also, those who depend on you have a tax-free death benefit.

LIFE INSURANCE POLICY

Life insurance is a protection against financial loss that results from the premature death of an insured. But there is a lot more that can be benefited from some type of insurance coverage. Life Insurance Policy is also beneficial because it can mimic the tax-free benefit of Roth without the downsides of limit on deposits. There are no contributions, no income limitations, and your expenses accrue to about 1½ per year.

INDEX UNIVERSAL INSURANCE

This is a permanent life insurance that can be used to accumulate wealth. It uses compound interest to potentially generate a large amount of non-taxable cash which can be accessed later in life to fund a happy retirement. It reflects stock market index performance while implementing a zero percent floor in the market gap.

There are different ways to approach index universal life insurance. **Whole life** is a type and it gives 5% returns, while **variable life** is another type which gives a higher level of returns with the market downside.

ORGANIZE YOUR FINANCES FOR RETIREMENT

- **List All Retirement Accounts**

    List your 401(k), 403(b), deferred comp plan, SEP,

SIMPLE, etc., or any personal retirement accounts such as an IRA. If you have an annuity that is titled as an IRA include it in this list.

If married, list your retirement accounts separately from your spouse's accounts. Also, if you have a Roth IRA or Designated Roth account through your employer, list those balances separately from your other retirement accounts.

- **Create A Net Worth Statement**

    You should list other savings and investment accounts, stocks, or bonds that are not owned inside of retirement accounts. Also, list other major assets such as your home, motorhome, other collectibles, etc. list only assets that are valuable. This net worth statement should be updated each year.

- **Income Timeline**

    When you retire, not all income sources start paying at the same time. You can intentionally delay when certain income should start, such as Social Security. An income timeline lays all this out for you allowing you to see what amount of your savings you may be required to fill in the gaps. Use the income timeline information to estimate income taxes that will be owed in retirement.

- **Spending Timeline**

    A spending timeline is a little different from a budget. It requires a budget, or list of all your expenses to complete your spending timeline.

    Project your expense items into the future. This is important because not all our expenses occur every year. The most common options that are missed on a retirement budget are Medicare Part B Premiums and other health care expenses, new car purchases, major home repairs, such as roof replacements, new carpeting, dental care, and the need for additional services such as a handyman, yard care, pool care, or home cleaning services.

- **Insurance Policies**

    Insurance policies need to be reviewed often, listing all by stating owner and policy number. Categorize your policies by property and casualty (homeowner, auto, etc.), life, health, disability, and long-term care. Review each category in light of your current goals and current pricing for that type of policy. Here are a few ideas to help you out.

INCREASE RETIREMENT SAVINGS

1. **Eliminate All Consumer Debt:** Credit card debt is wasteful and expensive. Pay off your highest interest balances first and use the money freed up as each card gets paid off to accelerate the payoff. Never spend more in a month than you can afford so you don't accumulate debt. Never settle for making minimum payments on credit cards because it's financial suicide on the installment plan. It makes compound interest work against you, instead of for you. The sooner you stop overspending and start paying down existing debt, the sooner that money can be redirected to investments, so that you're financing your retirement as a wealth builder instead of the bank executive's debtor.

2. **Increase Savings Automatically**: The least painful approach to lowering spending and increasing savings is with an automatic withdrawal plan from your paycheck. The small inconvenience of lower pay will be offset by the uplifting feeling of knowing that your retirement savings are back on track.

3. **Bank The Raise**: Most people increase expenses every time their income rises. Control spending by sending all raises and bonuses directly to savings where it can earn more income.

4. **Eliminate All Unnecessary Expenses:** A few dollars here and a few dollars there can add up to enormous sums today and compound into a fortune at retirement. The value of a $5 latte at age 40 can compound to over a $1,000 by the time you're in your 80s. A large part of our spending habits and new habits can be just as satisfying and a lot more enriching. Examine your expenses closely and get creative, because little differences in spending today can make a big difference in your retirement savings tomorrow.

5. **Consider New Employment**: The savings game is not about how much you earn, but how much you keep after taxes and expenses. One way to expand the gap between income and expenses is to consider new employment in another state or country where the cost of living is lower, allowing you to save more. Another possibility is to negotiate new employment with a company that would offer lucrative pension arrangements, thus taking the pressure off your savings.

6. **Moonlighting Income**: Second careers and home-based businesses have several advantages. The most obvious is they can provide additional income for your retirement savings. Less obvious is how they can safely transition you into a second career that

you might really enjoy continuing after retirement. Meanwhile, they can also open up the possibility of tax-deferred SEP and Keogh plans for self-employment retirement savings and other tax savings. The keys to making this strategy work are to pursue the moonlighting income in a field you're passionate about and would enjoy even during retirement, and to commit all revenue produced toward boosting savings rather than lifestyle. Always remember it's never too late to begin saving. Keep a positive focus, choose new habits that build savings, and you can achieve a comfortable retirement.

Retirement Savings Mistakes

The road to catching up on retirement savings is well-trodden. Many have made the journey before you and their experience teaches us where the most obvious potholes in the road are located. Anyone trying to catch-up on retirement savings faces certain obstacles and realities, making them susceptible to making the same mistakes. By learning about these common mistakes and avoiding them, you can save valuable time and money.

1. **Reaching For Return**:

    Don't ramp up portfolio risk in a desperate attempt to improve returns. You might luck out and enjoy magnified returns, but the odds favor something worse. Beware of investment scams, speculative stocks, viatical settlement deals, and anything else promising high returns with little or no risk. Be careful if it sounds too good to be true, it probably is.

2. **Assuming Overly Optimistic Returns:**

   Retirement planning would be a whole lot easier if we could push investment returns of 15% or more indefinitely into the future – but that's not a reality. Use conservative estimates so your retirement can be secure. Never use aggressive return estimates to force the numbers to work because running out of money in your old age is a tough price to pay for unrealistic assumptions.

3. **Eggs In One Basket**:

   Beware of investing too much of your 401(k) plan in company stock as you near retirement. A single company is much riskier than a diversified portfolio, and you can't afford the double whammy of losing your job and retirement savings at the same time should your company run into problems.

4. **Banking The Inheritance**:

   Many people use an expected inheritance as an excuse to not save for retirement. Life is uncertain.

The grantor could spend the inheritance on health care in their final years or make a foolish investment. A lot of things can go wrong and leave you empty-handed and destitute in your golden years if you don't take self-responsibility for your retirement savings.

5. **Don't Follow Simplistic Guidelines Blindly**:

   Retirement planning is an inexact process despite what all the experts may claim. You have unique skills, abilities, and interests that make you different from others. Your solution to catching up on retirement savings could look totally different from what your broker tells you. Just because he outlines asset allocation and savings requirements doesn't mean that you shouldn't go ahead and build that dream business or invest in real estate instead. It's your financial security. Consider all options and trust yourself to do what is uniquely right for your situation. You're the only one that has to live with the results.

6. **Invest For A Lifetime**:

   If you're 55 years young and planning to retire at 65, you should think twice about believing that your investment time horizon is just 10 years. If the odds are good and you expect to live at least another 30 years after retirement, lengthen your investment time frame to 40 years or more. Plan your investing accordingly and don't think too short-term.

7. **More Procrastination**:

What got you into this bind in the first place is procrastination, and what will get you out of it is doing the opposite. Get proactive by taking aggressive actions now to catch up on your retirement savings. The longer you wait, the harder it will be to catch up. There's no better time to get started than today.

Mindset Training:

The 'I'll Pay It Later' mindset is one that has placed so many people in debt troubles, because they are more concerned about later than they are about the here and now, and so they treat most of their present decisions and actions with levity.

The thing is if you can pay now, why choose to pay later?

Mindset training would point you towards the path of objective thinking and smarter decision making and not being confined to the 'herd effect', where one makes the decision to toe after others because others are taking a particular course of action.

It's always 'fatal' with finances.

CHAPTER 4

BALANCING PRESENT LIFESTYLE WITH THE FUTURE

Living in the present is no reason for one to fail to plan for a future that is sure to come, and planning for the future should not make you unable to take charge of your present either.

So, our living in the present should involve bridging the gaps between the present and the future.

If you find yourself feeling guilty about your lifestyle right now when you place it side by side with the picture of the future, then it is a sign you're not doing something right.

You need to do some balancing.

But then you don't have to live a miserable life in the present, starving yourself and pining away because you are securing your financial future. Don't forget that your tomorrow is not guaranteed and you could die before you get there.

This brings us to the point where we find and strike a balance between today and tomorrow, between living in the now as relating to the future.

Of course, money comes and goes, but time is an important resource that never comes around, and finding the balance between our present lifestyle and the future rests upon the time.

What we do with our time is the impact we will receive in the future.

There are things you could do for yourself now that you are younger which you cannot do for yourself when you get much older. When you have dreams that you' need to live out with the energy of your youth, live them out, but with thoughts about tomorrow to keep you in check.

The following practices would help you find the needed balance in your lifestyle, especially if you've not given them some thought yet:

In your retirement accounts, be sure to make your investments for the long term.

Make targeted savings for items you'll need so you won't have to over burn your income.

Set up a fitting retirement plan for yourself, one you will have to fall back on when you're too old to engage in active income generation.

Make sure not to take out money from your retirement plan too early over a whim or impulse to spend on the present.

Be careful how you make your expenses in the now so as to be able to have enough to spare and invest in the future.

When you earn bonuses on your income at the present, you may decide to give yourself some treats out of it and momentarily even out of financial restrictions. Life is for the living.

Have a bucket list of the things you want to achieve and to do with your life.

Keep a journal. It will make you aware of everything that matters, inclusive of situations that won't readily come to mind without a reminder. This will help you keep in mind and in constant focus the things that are really important, and by so doing, position you better for the future.

CHAPTER 5

BUCKET LIST

Importance of having a bucket list:

A bucket list summarily is a list of your dreams and intended achievements before you kick the bucket. It is a list that you make with the intention of keeping your dreams and your goals alive.

The items on the list must not come in a particular order, as their purpose is to motivate you, and the essence of writing them down is to boost your confidence thereby making your list more real to you.

Your list must not be filled with gigantic tasks, that you'll end up not satisfactorily fulfilling even one out of, make sure they are things you could eventually achieve.

Ticking off your list with time will give you the uplifting sense of accomplishment and eventually help you make the best of your time, and of your life, by giving you direction, purpose, and focus.

I highlight some important questions for those who are retired:

Who are you?

Where do you want to go?

What do you want to do when you retire? if you want it to become a reality and not just a fantasy or wish list you need a strategy for goal achievement.

Who do you want to go with?

What accomplishments do you want during retirement?

Why do you want to go?

What moves you?

Review each retirement question and put your answer below.

Plans to pursue during retirement may include:

- Self-discovery: know your interests, likes, dislikes, and limitations.

- Emphasize pursuit of your dreams.

- Ensure your life activities matter.

- Treat nutrition and fitness as important.

- Involve in some hobbies and activities with your spouse.

- Become a mentor; pass a skill or hobby to a younger friend.

- Give some of your time back to the community.

- Take a course.

- Write a commentary on a topic of interest. Read plenty of new material.

- Go on a cruise.

- Volunteer for charity.

- Run a marathon.

- Grow vegetables / start a garden.
- Travel across the world.
- Fly in a helicopter.
- Learn a foreign language.
- Try an extreme sport, such as skydiving.
- Learn to play the piano / other musical instruments.
- Go horseback riding.
- Renew your wedding vows.
- Whale and dolphin watching.
- Visit distant friends or relatives.
- Fix up a classic car or motorcycle.
- Work on the family tree/track down long-lost family.
- Ride an elephant, hot air balloon.
- Sell something you have made yourself.
- Go to a concert of a favorite band/singer.
- Take dancing lessons.

- Try yoga.

This is just a list to guide you to choose based on what interests you. The key to having a healthy retirement and enjoying yourself in the process, is staying busy.

CHAPTER 6

WHAT WE'VE BEEN TAUGHT, AGAINST WHAT IS TRUE:

Most of the time, we find that what we grew up believing to be true turns out being deeply seated perceptions and beliefs of the individuals who thought us these things, which in most cases doesn't work for everyone, or are absolutely wrong.

Putting an end to these myths, misconceptions, and theoretical inaccuracies is the beginning of self-discovery; for every life and in every field of endeavor.

These include among many others:

Invest in what's trending based on current returns: this myth is all about emphasizing on the short term and in the present. But the fact is that what is trending now may likely not be in existence in the next few years. The best option is to diversify in the short term and invest in the long term.

Investing more conservatively close to retirement: out of fear, so many misses out on great business opportunities because they believe they would lose money should they invest aggressively towards their retirement. But the truth is, aggressive investment will in the long run yield greater returns and will work for you while you take care of other things in your retirement.

Spending less on taxes when retired: the truth is that if in retirement, your income remains at the same rate as it was while you were actively working, there's no guarantee that you will pay lesser tax. On the contrary, you may end up paying a higher prevalent tax rate if you had failed to secure smarter investments or savings while you worked.

CHAPTER 7

MASTERY OVER YOUR FINANCE

Commit to paying yourself a percentage of your income towards your freedom funds.

Become an investor, put some money aside for your investment and don't touch it.

Know the rules: everything in life has principles and rules that determine your success or failure. Therefore, before getting in, know the rules such as; consider a fiduciary instead of a broker because they are bound by law to work in your best interest, take little risks that bring great rewards.

Determine your risk tolerance and invest correctly and smartly.

Invest like a billionaire: don't lose money, seek asymmetrical risk and reward, anticipate financial risk, diversify income and have a continuous hunger for knowledge.

Enjoy your money and life.

Levels of financial freedom

- Financial security: just getting by
- Financial vitality
- Financial independence
- Financial freedom
- Absolute freedom

Moving Up The Financial Ladder

- Earn more money and invest the difference.
- Reduce fees and taxes.
- Save more money.
- Maximize returns on investment.

- Alter your lifestyle and invest the difference.

Invest in creating the retirement you desire by taking the right steps, live with the future in mind, commit to giving yourself a retirement that rewards all your hard work.

www.ingramcontent.com/pod-product-compliance
Lightning Source LLC
Chambersburg PA
CBHW050028230526
45470CB00003B/1175